Whales

Killer Whales, Blue Whales and More

Written by Deborah Hodge

Illustrated by Pat Stephens

KIDS CAN PRESS

WILDLIFE SERIES

Kids Can Press

For my parents, Marion and Lyndon – DH
For Doug, Carrie, Mom and Jamie – PS

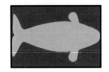

I would like to gratefully acknowledge the expert review of the text and illustrations by Dr. John Ford, Ph.D., Marine Mammal Scientist, Vancouver Public Aquarium in Stanley Park, Vancouver, B.C., Canada.

I would also like to thank my editor, Valerie Wyatt, for her wisdom and humor, and my publishers, Valerie Hussey and Ricky Englander, for providing me with the opportunity to create the Wildlife Series.

Thanks are also due to my friend and colleague, Linda Bailey.

Text copyright © 1997 by Deborah Hodge
Illustrations copyright © 1997 by Pat Stephens

Published in Canada by
Kids Can Press Ltd.
29 Birch Avenue
Toronto, ON M4V 1E2

Published in the U.S. by
Kids Can Press Ltd.
85 River Rock Drive, Suite 202
Buffalo, NY 14207

Edited by Valerie Wyatt
Designed by Marie Bartholomew
Printed in Hong Kong by Wing King Tong Co.Ltd.

CMC 97 0 9 8 7 6 5 4 3 2
CMC PA 98 0 9 8 7 6 5 4 3 2

Canadian Cataloguing in Publication Data

Hodge, Deborah
    Whales : killer whales, blue whales and more

(Kids Can Press wildlife series)
Includes index.
ISBN 1-55074-356-2 (bound)
ISBN 1-55074-418-6 (pbk.)

1. Whales — Juvenile literature. I. Stephens, Pat.
II. Title. III. Series.

QL737.C4H63 1996   j599.5   C96-930472-2

Contents

Whales

Whales are big wild animals that live in the ocean. They are sometimes called the giants of the sea.

Whales look like huge fish, but they are mammals. Like other mammals, they breathe with lungs and they are warm-blooded. Their body temperature stays warm, even in cold water. Mammal babies feed on their mother's milk.

Blue whales are the biggest animals in the world. They can grow as long as a train car — up to 30 m (100 feet) long! A newborn Blue whale is as long as a school bus.

Narwhal: 4.5 m (15 feet)

A Killer whale has sharp teeth for grabbing prey.

Long-finned pilot whale: 7m (23 feet)

Sperm whale: 18 m (60 feet)

Baleen whales

Most of the big whales are baleen whales. Instead of teeth, baleen whales have long fringes called baleen. The baleen is used to strain food out of the water. Baleen whales have two blowholes for breathing. Female baleen whales are usually bigger than the males.

Blue whale: 26 m (85 feet)

Humpback whale: 15 m (49 feet)

Northern right whale: 17 m (55 feet)

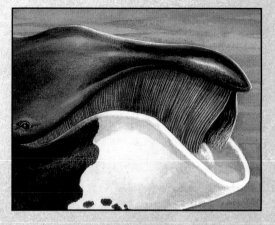

This Bowhead whale is showing its baleen. It has the longest baleen of any whale.

Pacific gray whale: 14 m (46 feet)

Bowhead whale: 18 m (60 feet)

Fin whale: 22 m (73 feet)

9

Where whales live

Whales live in the ocean. The ocean provides food for the whales, and the water holds up their heavy bodies. There are whales in all the oceans of the world.

Some whales live mainly in the oceans around North America. They include the Gray whale, Bowhead whale, Northern right whale, Long-finned pilot whale, Beluga and Narwhal.

Baleen whales, such as this Fin whale, often live alone.

Beluga whales
live in larger
groups than most
other whales. At
feeding times,
pods of a
thousand or more
Belugas may
swim together.

Most toothed whales live in groups called pods.
A pod of 12 to 20 whales swims together and
searches for food. Some toothed whales, such
as these Belugas, swim in even bigger groups.
Belugas hunt for fish in the icy waters of the Arctic.

Why whales migrate

Most baleen whales swim to warm waters for winter and cool waters for summer. This is called migrating. Whales migrate to warm oceans to give birth to their babies. They swim back to cool oceans to feed. Baleen whales migrate farther than any other mammals in the world.

Every fall, Gray whales migrate from the cold Arctic to the ocean off Mexico. In these warm waters, they rest and have their babies. They return to Arctic feeding grounds in the spring. In a year, a Gray whale may swim up to 16 000 km (10 000 miles).

WHALE FACT

The bumps on a Gray whale's skin are small animals called barnacles and whale lice.

Where Gray whales migrate

Arctic Ocean

Canada

U.S.A.

Pacific
Ocean

Mexico

Calves are born here

Whale bodies

This Fin whale is a baleen whale. Its body is built for life in the ocean.

Baleen

Baleen whales have baleen — rows of long fringes that fit together like teeth in a comb. The whale uses its baleen to strain food from the water. Toothed whales have teeth instead of baleen.

Blowholes

A whale breathes through blowholes that lead to its lungs.

Fins

The whale uses its fins to steer.

Throat grooves

Folds under the Fin whale's jaw push out during feeding. Its throat becomes a huge container for water and food. Only some whales have these throat grooves.

Bones

A whale's bones are very light. Its skeleton does not need to be strong and heavy because the water holds up the whale's weight.

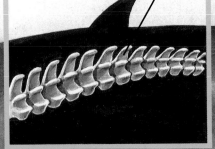

Tail and flukes

The whale's tail has very strong muscles. The whale pushes its tail up and down to swim. The curved ends are called flukes.

Skin and blubber

A whale has smooth skin to help it glide through the water. A layer of body fat under the skin is called blubber. Blubber keeps the whale warm and serves as food when the whale is not eating.

How whales move

Whales are strong swimmers. They move by pumping their powerful tails up and down. As well as swimming underwater, whales also jump and splash at the surface. These Humpback whales are doing some common whale moves.

Some whales poke their heads out of the water to look around. This is called **spyhopping**.

This Humpback whale is **breaching** — leaping up and splashing down. Scientists aren't sure why whales breach. Perhaps they are playing.

WHALE FACT

Humpback whales are the most acrobatic of all whales.

Some whales slap their flippers on the water's surface. A **flipper slap** may be a way of sending a message to other whales.

When whales slap their tails on the water, it is called **tail slapping**. A tail slap makes a loud noise. It may mean the whale is angry.

Whale sounds

Toothed whales make clicking sounds. The clicks echo off objects in the water. The whales use the echoes to find their food and steer through the dark ocean.

Scientists think that whales make other sounds to "talk" to one another. Fin whales moan, Belugas chirp and Humpback whales sing.

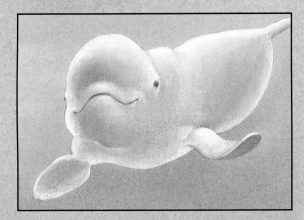

Sailors once called Belugas "sea canaries" because they make such loud chirping sounds.

Like humans, Killer whales have dialects. This means that each pod has a slightly different way of "speaking."

Every pod of Killer whales has about ten special calls. Scientists learn about a pod's habits by listening to the calls through underwater microphones.

Whale food

What a whale eats depends on its mouth.

Toothed whales eat fish and squid. They chase their prey through the water and swallow them in one big gulp.

This Sperm whale may dive down 1000 m (3280 feet) or more to catch a giant squid.

Baleen whales eat krill and plankton — tiny plants and animals that float in the water. They also eat small fish swimming in schools.

This Right whale feeds by swimming with its mouth open. As it swims, water and krill flow into the whale's mouth. The water washes out through the baleen, but the krill stays trapped inside.

This is a close-up of the krill that many Baleen whales eat. Some krill are smaller than a grain of rice.

How whales are born

A whale baby, called a calf, is born under water. Seconds after it is born, the mother helps it to the surface so that it can breathe. The mother watches closely over her new calf. She protects it from danger.

The whale calf stays near its mother and drinks her rich milk. The milk is full of fat and helps the calf grow quickly.

This Sperm whale mother squeezes out her milk. The baby gulps it down.

A Killer whale calf is born tail first. The calf is about 2 m (6 feet) long — as long as a couch. Being big helps a newborn whale survive in the cold ocean water.

How whales grow and learn

Hours after it is born, a whale calf can swim well. Soon it will learn to breach and dive.

Most whale calves stay with their mother until she is ready to give birth to a new baby — up to two or three years. It may take ten or more years for the young whale to reach full size.

A Humpback mother and her calf swim close together. They touch each other often.

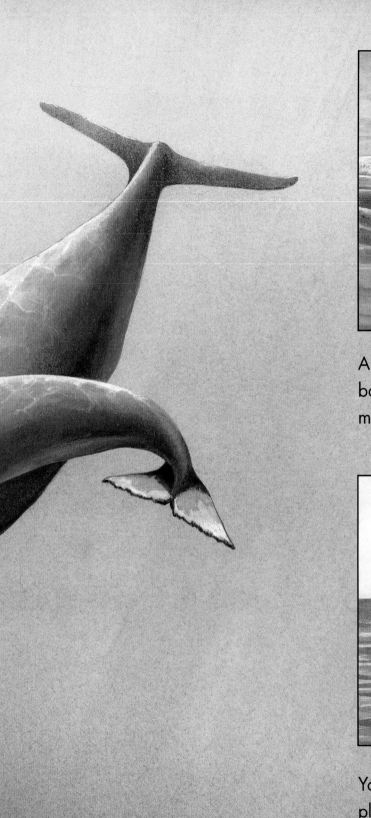

A new calf tires easily. This baby Gray whale rests on its mother's back.

Young Killer whales like to play. They practice breaching and diving.

How whales protect themselves

Whales are huge animals, so they fear few creatures. Killer whales and sharks are the only wild enemies that whales have. Killer whales will attack almost anything that swims — including whales much bigger than themselves.

Gray whales hide in a kelp forest. The kelp protects them from Killer whales, who send out clicking sounds to find their prey. The clicks bounce off the kelp instead of the Gray whales. They are safe!

Whales and people

Years ago, whales were hunted all over the world. Now there are laws to protect them. Sadly, some whales, such as the Right whale and the Blue whale, were hunted so much that there are very few left today.

Like all living creatures, whales need food, clean air and water. When oil or other harmful things spill into the ocean, the whales' food may be spoiled or killed. Whales depend on clean oceans and lots of food to live and be healthy.

Sometimes Pilot whales swim up on
shore. Scientists don't know why.
People try to rescue the whales by
helping them back into the water.

Whale watching

Today many people watch whales instead of hunting them. To tell whales apart, people look at the size and shape of a whale's body, its coloring and markings. Some people also look at tail size and shape.

Blue whale

Humpback whale

Killer whale

Gray whale

Narwhal

Sperm whale

Compare the whale's tail that spreads across these two pages with the ones on the left. Can you figure out which type of whale it is?

It is a Blue whale. In real life its tail would be 15 times bigger than the tail you see on these two pages.

Words to know

baleen: rows of long, bristly fringes through which a whale strains its food

baleen whale: a whale with baleen instead of teeth

blow: a big puff of air that a whale breathes out

blowhole: an opening in the top of a whale's head through which the whale breathes

blubber: a thick layer of body fat under the skin

calf: a young whale

krill: tiny shrimp-like creatures that baleen whales eat

mammal: a warm-blooded animal whose babies are born live and drink their mother's milk. Mammals have lungs for breathing.

migrate: to travel from one place to another as the seasons change

plankton: tiny plants and animals that float together in the ocean

pod: a group of whales that swim together and search for food

prey: an animal that is hunted for food

toothed whale: a whale with teeth instead of baleen

warm-blooded: having a warm body temperature, even when the air or water is cold

Index